I am
Albert Einstein

I am
Albert Einstein

By Renee A. Irene

Illustrated by Sophia Ian

I am Albert Einstein

A collection of biographies from the *Who Am I Series* an OPEN UNIVERSAL LIBRARY biography

PUBLISHED 2017
by Open Universal Library.
First Edition.

ISBN: 978-1544259406

Also by Open Universal Library:

I am Barack Obama
I am Muhammad Ali
I am Walt Disney
I am Justin Bieber
I am Donald Trump
I am LeBron James
I am Leonardo Da Vinci

www.openuniversallibrary.com

Contents

Prologue

In 1955, a lot of things happened for America. The first episode of The Mickey Mouse Club aired on television. The first Guinness Book of Records was published. Disneyland opened in California. The musical Peter Pan was broadcast live on television. But amongst all these good things, an event took place that was not only a loss for America but for the rest of the world as well. Albert Einstein, probably the greatest

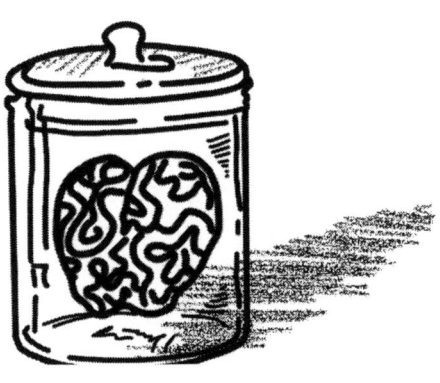

scientist of the century, passed away. He was the man whose discoveries created the basis for modern physics. Thanks to Einstein, we have invented lasers, satellites and mobile phones. His work is still important today and will continue to be so for generations to come. However, the most remarkable thing about this man that the whole world mourned was his personality. Einstein was not afraid of speaking his mind. He was the man who warned President Roosevelt about the dangers of nuclear weapons, the man who was offered the second presidency of Israel and turned it down. The man who, when faced with paparazzi photographers, stuck his tongue out at them, resulting in the most iconic picture of this amazing personality, and the man whose brain is now located at the Princeton University Medical Center.

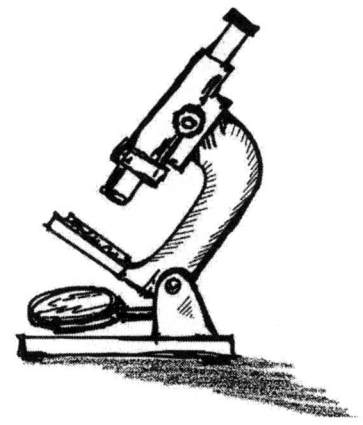

Chapter I
The Man who Revolutionized Physics as We Know It

Albert Einstein, the man who revolutionized the laws of life, had a humble beginning to his own life in Ulm, Germany. He was the first child of Hermann and Pauline Einstein and was born three years after their marriage, on 14 March, 1879. They spent only a short time in Ulm, as they moved to Munich in 1880, where Albert's father founded an electrical engineering company called Einstein & Cie with his brother Jakob. For an exceptional man, Albert's childhood was quite mundane and, to the disappointment of his family, he did not start speaking until quite late. He began playing the violin in 1885, which he continued for six years with the support of his mother, who was herself a talented musician.

It was at around the age of four or five that the greatest physicist of the 20th century was first exposed to a scientific experiment, with a compass shown to him by his father. The young Einstein was awed by the mechanics of the simple compass which constantly pointed north and his fascination with science began

there and then. By the age of six he had started learning to play the piano and began to attend a Catholic elementary school, the Petersschule on Munich's Blumenstrasse. Even though they were Jewish, his parents cared more about the curriculum than the school's religious affiliation. Albert's academic performance in the field of science was a premonition of his future success. However, he found it hard to mix with the other pupils and to cope with the school's staunch

principles and discipline. Instead, he preferred to spend time playing with his sister Maria who was about two years his junior.

His pedantic family was ecstatic when the ten-year-old Albert was accepted at the formal and prestigious Luitpold Gymnasium in Munich. But to Albert's dismay, the curriculum, which included a great deal of Greek and Latin, did not really correspond to his taste for science. He was an unhappy pupil until he found an outlet with a twenty-one-year-old medical student called

Max Talmud, who lent him books on science and philosophy. He endured his new school by solving math's puzzles on the side until his father and uncle decided to move to the south of Italy. Arrangements were made for Albert to stay at the Luitpold Gymnasium School as a boarder in order to finish his studies, but within six months he persuaded a doctor to sign him off with neurasthenic exhaustion. There are two theories as to why he eventually moved from Munich to Italy. Firstly, that he was dissatisfied

with the education given at his school and secondly, that according to German law, if he left before the age of seventeen he would not be obliged to do military service.

Surprisingly, at the age of eleven, Albert went through a critical religious phase and tried hard to demonstrate his belief in God by composing hymns to the glory of the Lord, observing all the Kosher laws and even reading the Bible with great diligence. But as his understanding of science progressed he became

weary of religion and any other dogmas that could hinder his creativity in the realms of science. Not long after arriving in Pavia, the future physicist dismayed his parents by renouncing both his Jewish religion and his German nationality. His reason for this was so that he could experience the freedom and isolation he had always desired. Dedicated to pursuing what enthralled him the most, he prepared for the entrance examination to the Swiss Federal Polytechnic School, which he failed the first time due to not reaching

the required standard in subjects other than mathematics. But then, following the advice of the principal of the Polytechnic, he enrolled at the secondary school in Aarau in Northern Switzerland and prepared for the exam again. By the time his secondary schooling was over, around 1896, Einstein was a self-assured, confident, and relatively communicative individual.

Einstein immediately enrolled at the Institute he had prepared for with one goal in mind – to become a mathematics and physics teacher. As soon as he obtained his diploma in 1900, he applied for vacancies as assistant teacher at various universities, but all in vain. Meanwhile, his Swiss citizenship came through in February, 1901. His struggles with unemployment also paid off the same year when he found a job at the Winterthur and Schaffhausen technical school as a teacher. He remained there until 1902, when he moved to the capital city, Bern. At about this point in time he founded the "Olympia Academy" with two other people in order to make a living from tutoring. They devised a strategy whereby lectures in mathematics and physics were given in the mornings and healthy discussions about philosophy and science took place in the evenings. Einstein had also applied for a position in the Bernese patent-office and in

1903 he became a technical expert. Despite the workload, he was still able to find time for his research into theoretical physics.

Chapter 2
Juggling Science and Family

Not so long ago, in the 1980s, the physicist's private letters fell into the hands of the public, revealing that he had a daughter from an affair in 1902, the year that he moved to Bern. Einstein's daughter and one of his fellow students (Mileva Maric) disappeared. Nothing is known of the child except for her name, Lieserl, who according to the most widespread rumor, was put up for adoption. Following his father's death in 1902, Einstein married Mileva in 1903, even though both their families were opposed to the idea. In the following year his first son, Hans

Albert, was born, while his second son, Eduard, was born in 1910.

During his student years at the Polytechnic, Einstein fell in love with Mileva and the two continued to grow closer. They kept in contact via letters, in which he expressed many of his scientific ideas. Mileva, who was also very interested in mathematics and physics, is believed to have greatly influenced Einstein's theories, including his famous theory of relativity. It is said that they naturally exchanged ideas

when discussing his work, but there is no written proof of her contribution. Mileva's intellectual and personal relationship with Einstein may well have played a role in his successful career, but this is mere speculation. In any case, the couple was not destined to last forever. According to a visitor, their house was always untidy and even though Albert would try to help out, he was not really committed to domestic duties and he would end up just carrying the baby while trying to write equations on his notepad. Things did not improve with time and the couple started to drift apart soon after Einstein moved to Berlin in 1914, to take up a place at the University of Berlin. At the same time as his professional success grew, his marriage deteriorated and ended in divorce in 1919. Mileva moved back to Zurich with her sons and Einstein stayed in Berlin with his family, only to remarry, the very same year he was divorced, his cousin, Elsa Lowenthal, whom he had come to love.

His former wife lived in decent

circumstances thanks to Einstein's promise to give her all the money he received from the Nobel Prize he won in 1921. She successfully invested it

all in real estate, but was forced to sell it in later years in order to cope with the high costs incurred by her younger son's mental illness. Eduard was a gifted child, eager to learn and with a photographic memory, but he was mentally unstable and had to be placed in a psychiatric hospital in 1933. Hans, the older son, married and

moved to the United States, but Mileva continued to care for her beloved Eduard until she died in 1948.

Elsa was Albert's maternal aunt's daughter. A divorcee, she lived in the apartment above her parents' home in Berlin with her two daughters. After Einstein moved there they often saw each other and Einstein felt comfortable with her. Soon after his divorce from Mileva he felt free to marry Elsa, but their marriage was a platonic one, with little passion. However, unlike the disorderly living conditions that Einstein had faced in his first marriage, Elsa was very efficient in running the household, giving Einstein the

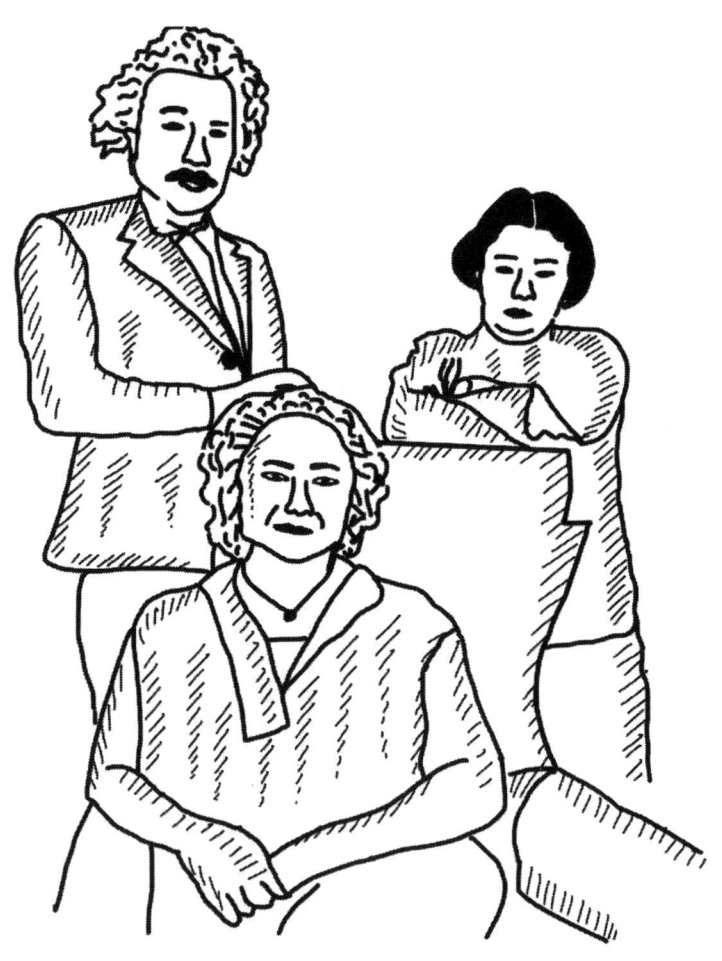

good food of which he was fond and a pleasant environment to work in. Nevertheless, despite having a healthy marriage, Einstein continued to flirt with other women and this caused problems with Elsa, as it had done with Mileva. In 1935, when they moved to America, Elsa fell ill and died a year later. Einstein was very attentive and caring during her last days.

Chapter 3
The Miracle Year

During the years when Einstein worked in the Bernese Patent-office, he had spare time in which he cemented his theories of physics. Unlike his time at the Polytechnics when everything was at hold because of his studies. Slowly developing his ideas he hit jackpot in 1905 when he published four papers which changed physics for the world. It is thus known as the miracle year because of four theorems that proved to be so solid that they were groundbreaking for physicists around the world. In that time, Annalen der Physic, one of the best physics journals presented the theory of photoelectric

effect, the Brownian motion, the special theory of relativity and the matter/energy relationship and gave physics a new identity.

In the photoelectric effect he presented the idea of light coming in chunks of energy and not as a single beam. This was very different from the classical theory which stated that light was a wave rather than particles travelling together. The chunks were called photons of light individually. The photoelectric effect stated that some lights like the blue light have more energy in comparison to the other lights such as red light in each of their photons. So whenever blue light hits the surface of a metal it carries enough energy in a single photon to release one electron from the metal itself. But when red light hits the surface it cannot have the same reaction regardless of the intensity of the light. Because by increasing intensity you're increasing the number of photons hit the surface but the energy level in each photon remains the

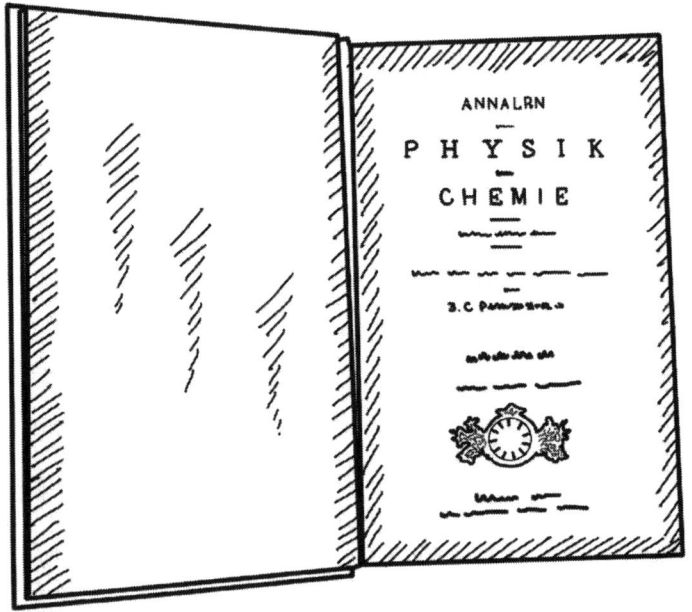

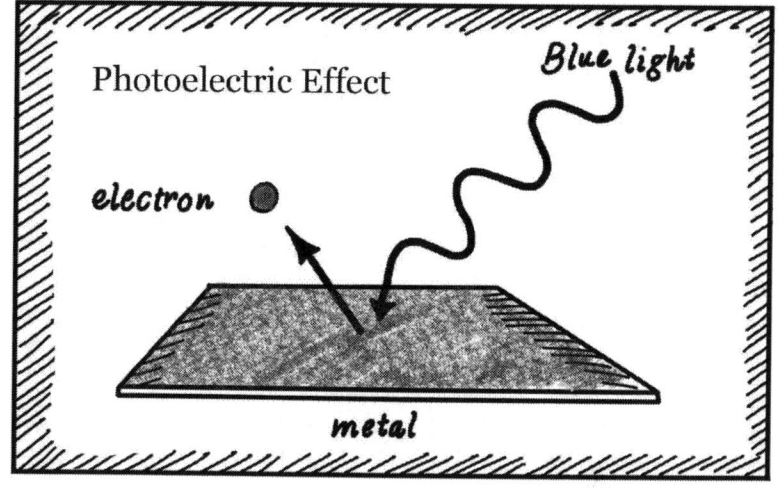

Photoelectric Effect

Blue light

electron

metal

same i.e. not enough to free the electron from its bond.

The Brownian motion is a simpler concept that discusses the random movement of particles because they constantly collide with the particles of the medium they are sustained in. To make it easier for understanding one may imagine pollen grains in a glass beaker half filled with water, the pollen grains hardly ever stays still, in fact they don't. They move about randomly in multiple directions because they constantly hit

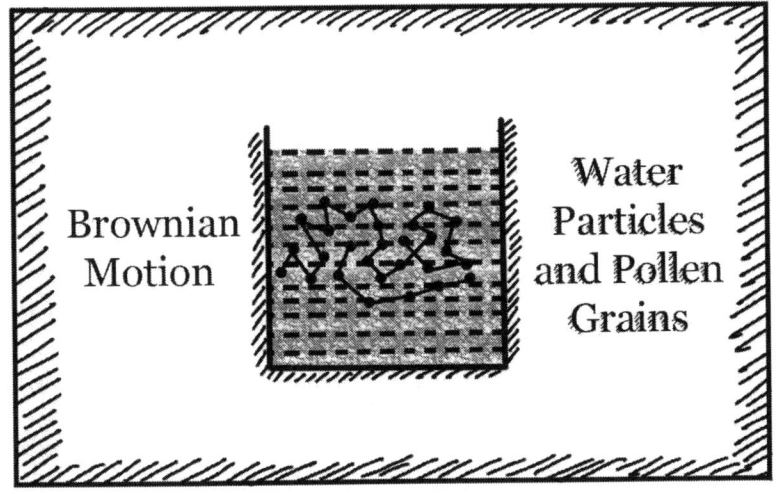

Brownian Motion — Water Particles and Pollen Grains

they water particles and hence are thrown in a new direction.

The special theory of relativity states that the speed of light is the same for all observers. As stated by the formula Speed= Distance/Time distance and time differ accordingly to keep the speed of light the same.

This is made possible by the concept of time elongation, for the things that were seemingly near. It would seem that light coming from that point would reach before, in such cases the time seems to slow down a little so the light could travel at the same speed but reach in exactly the same time as the light coming from a distance. Then there is distance contraction for the things coming from afar in comparison, so that it would travel with the same speed but reach in exactly the same time as the light that has a shorter distance to cover from the start.

Taking this concept further Einstein presented the idea of time travel. Since by his logic, for anything travelling near the speed of

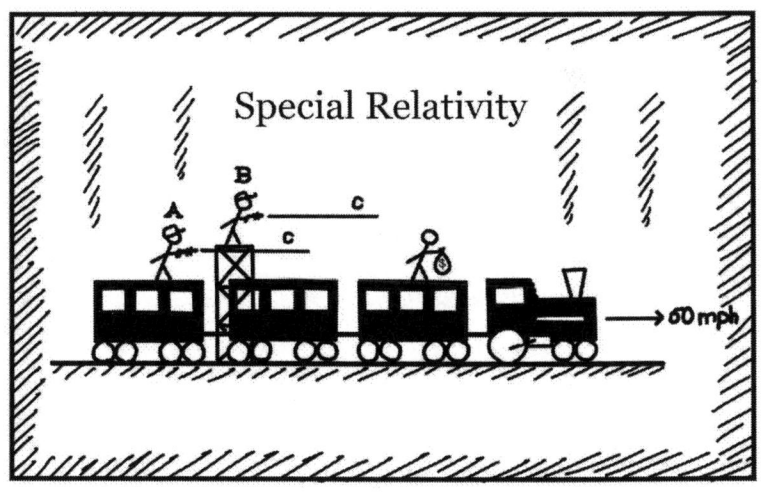

$$E = mc^2$$

light time slows down until it gradually reaches the speed of light. That is when time comes to a halt for that object. What happens when you travel faster than the speed of light? Yes, time will move backwards of you, making you a time traveler. Sadly, no one has been able to achieve that level of speed till now.

In his last paper where he discussed matter/energy relationships, Einstein made his most circulated and famous equation $E=mc^2$. It suggested that matter can be converted into huge amounts of energy and it foreshadowed all nuclear energy development, it is still used to get an estimate of the amount of energy released or consumed by nuclear reactions. It concluded that whenever energy will be released or consumed it will be in the form of light or heat. This explains why nuclear weapons produce such a massive amount of energy.

All of his theories were supported by a well-renowned Quantum theorist of that time, Max Planck. Einstein because an instant star in the academia circuit and was offered many jobs which he took before finally becoming the director of Kaiser Wilhelm Institute for Physics in 1913.

Chapter 4
The Great Debate

In 1915, Einstein hit another physics gold mine when he discovered that extremely large objects in the vacuum of space (such as the Earth and the Sun) cause a curve to appear in the space-time continuum. Imagine a huge trampoline with a heavy ball in its center, creating a dip. Now if you push a marble onto the trampoline it will spin around the ball in an orbiting kind of motion. In other words, the idea is that large bodies in space-time attract others around them. This was the basis of Einstein's idea of gravity in his Theory of General Relativity completed in 1915.

This was a groundbreaking discovery which took the entire world by storm, with the exception of the Nobel Committee. By this time Einstein had a long history of Nobel Prize nominations, but as in previous years, the Committee once again decided not to award him the Nobel Prize. Their reason for this was simple - that his theory of relativity was unproven. The theory needed to be confirmed for it to be accepted for the Nobel Prize. Soon afterwards, in 1919, an astrophysicist from Cambridge

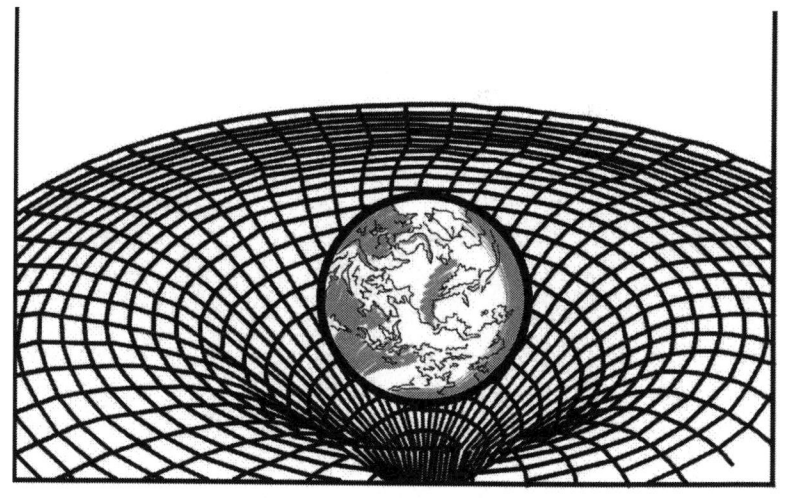

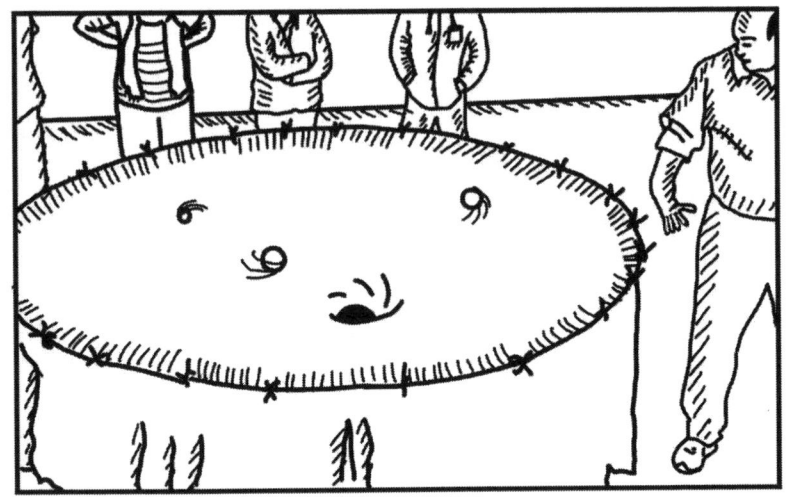

called Arthur Eddington proved it, by matching the values of one of his own experiments with the values predicted by Einstein.

Nevertheless Einstein did not receive the award this time either and for reasons that were more sinister. Hatred towards Jews was rising in Germany and Einstein, with his Jewish background and his stance against war and violence, was an obvious target. The crisis reached its peak in 1921, when the Committee decided not to award any Nobel Prize for Physics since "nobody" was eligible. Arguments followed for an entire year and the Committee eventually reached a compromise. Einstein was awarded a Nobel Prize but for his Theory of Photoelectric Effect and not for his Theory of General Relativity. And when receiving the award, he was told that it was given to him without taking into consideration the value that would be given to his Theory of General Relativity, if and when it was proven in the future.

Einstein was not at all happy with this, for two reasons. First, because the Theory of Photoelectric Effect was from his 1905 paper and he believed that the Theory of General Relativity was going to have a greater impact on the world. Second, because it had indeed been proven and was a legitimate theory with a proper foundation. However, the Committee

argued that when carrying out his research, the astrophysicist had not paid enough attention to information that he considered to be inadequate. Furthermore, he was not even present in the country to receive his award even though he had been informed beforehand of the prize-giving ceremony. In any case, the prize had already lost its charm for Einstein. The German Foreign Minister had been killed and, during

NOBEL

— PRIZE —

WINNER

the subsequent investigation, it was discovered that Einstein's name was included in the list of potential targets. To avoid the problems involved with attending the ceremony, he left for Japan instead to give a tour of lectures. However, even though relativity was not the reason for his Nobel Prize, Einstein still chose to talk about it in his acceptance speech.

The Nobel Prize concerned more than just Einstein's reputation, or the Committee's authority. It closely affected the wellbeing of his former wife and two sons. As Germany entered World War I, inflation skyrocketed. So in the end, the money was the best part about winning, as it not only helped his former family to live a decent life, but it also helped with his son Eduard's treatment when he developed a mental disorder as a young adult.

Chapter 5
A Nationality Crisis

"I shall become a Swiss Jew for the Germans, and a German man of Science for the English."

- Albert Einstein

Einstein's disagreement with Germany started in his teens, owing to his political views about peace which clashed with Germany's military regime. He wanted to stay as far away from any military involvement as possible. In order to avoid serving time in the German army, he left the country before the age of 17, after which it would have been mandatory to join up for a certain length of time. He also forsook his

German nationality in 1896 and never regretted it.

Einstein's political views were always in favor of peace and he was vehemently opposed to accepting any kind of domination. He moved to Switzerland, which is possibly the most diplomatic state in the world, and in 1899, while he was a student in Zurich, applied for Swiss citizenship. But like his job, this did not materialize overnight. It took two years before his request was approved, when with a legal fee

of 600 Swiss Francs he became a Swiss citizen.

In 1913, he received an offer from Berlin that was too tempting to ignore, but he nevertheless made one condition before accepting it and this was that he would be allowed to keep his Swiss nationality. This was granted and Einstein worked in Berlin as a Swiss citizen and never notified the police before leaving the country as all foreigners were supposed to do. When World War I broke out, he managed to avoid German military obligations thanks to his Swiss citizenship. However, despite not keeping his German citizenship, he was respected and welcomed by the German people, due to the impending fame and prestige they thought he would bring to Germany, which indeed he did. All the while he emphasized that he was a Swiss citizen, paid army exemption tax to Switzerland and renewed his residence permit in Germany

on a regular basis.

It was the German government's idea in 1922 that the Swiss embassy should apply on Einstein's behalf for a permanent German visa to reduce the cost incurred every time it was renewed. So even in the eyes of the German

government, the professor was Swiss. But they also declared that his work was an integral part of German research, and that he was one of the only Germans to be welcomed by other nations. With Einstein's growing international fame, Germany's desire to claim him as one of its own people also increased.

The actual crisis occurred when Einstein was awarded a Nobel Prize and was not there to receive it because of his lecture tour. Who would receive it on his behalf? In a hurried and confused debate, it was concluded that he was given the award as a scientific figure, and as his research largely depended on Germany, he was considered to be a "German" scientist. It was consequently decided that the award would be

received by a German representative. However, the decision soon became embarrassing, as not only was Einstein still travelling on his Swiss passport, he also never showed any recognition of being a German citizen or any inclination to be one. In the end they decided to turn a hasty mistake into an official fact. While his

Swiss citizenship was not to be affected he would be treated as a German citizen as well. This became official in February 1924 but he continued to travel on his Swiss passport until 1925, when the Swiss government (still bitter about the Nobel Prize incident) turned down his request for a diplomatic passport. The German government gratefully filled the gap and from then on he travelled on his German passport.

Chapter 6
Traveling the World

Einstein's achievements are not limited to four famous scientific papers. Although they certainly stand out and represent what he is most famous for, he was not just known for physics. He published other works, for example "About Zionism", "Why War?", "My Philosophy" and "Out of My Later Years". Einstein received honorary doctorates from different universities in Philosophy, Medicine and Science. His IQ level ranged from 160 to 190, the normal IQ range being between 85 and 115.

During the year of the Nobel Prize debate, Einstein traveled abroad on many study tours.

His first but not last visit to the United States was in April of that same year. The tour lasted three weeks, during which Einstein gave multiple lectures in different universities, including Princeton and Columbia University. He visited the White House with a delegation from the National Academy of Science during his trip and

in an essay about his tour, he openly admitted to liking the American people. After that he went to England to visit Viscount Haldane, who was a philosopher in London. Not only did Einstein meet people of great stature and intellect in his time there, but he also delivered a lecture at King's College London.

When the Nobel Prize was finally awarded to Einstein he was in Asia delivering lectures. He visited Singapore before going on to Ceylon and Japan, where he met the Emperor and the Empress. In one of his letters, he told his son about his fascination with the Japanese, commenting that he found them to be self-sufficient, humble and bright and that they knew the spirit of art. His travels then led him to Palestine. With his wife Elsa he visited Israel before it became a state, visiting the new Jewish Yishuv, which was basically Jewish people building houses outside the walls of Jerusalem before the State of Israel was created. They welcomed him wholeheartedly in the presence of their Head of State, with a cannon salute and

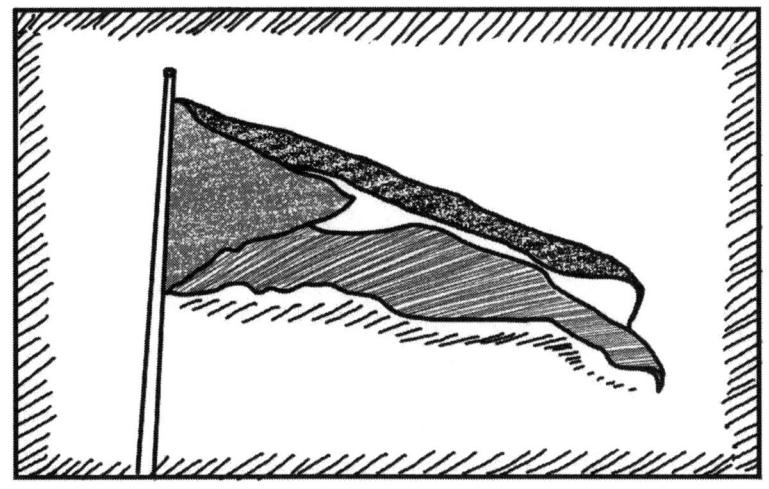

the crowd singing "Here comes the Messiah". During his 12-day stay, there were swarms of people who wanted to see him and hear him talk.

However in 1929, Einstein wrote in a letter to his friend Chaim Weizmann (who later became Israel's first president) that he felt that some sort of compromise should be made with the Arabs of Palestine and that a separate state for Jews was not the right answer.

Despite all that, in 1952, many years after

his visit and while he was in America, the Minister of the Israeli Embassy in the U.S. handed him a letter offering him the Presidency of Israel. Accepting it included the condition of moving to Israel and taking up Israeli citizenship in addition to many other regulations. They proposed that he continue carrying out all his scientific work at the expense of the government. Einstein humbly but firmly declined the offer, on the basis of his inability to mix with other people or to follow strict official rules. He declared that he would be unsuitable for the post and felt scared and stressed at the idea, because his bond with his Jewish brothers had strengthened since becoming aware of the unstable position of Jews in the world.

Chapter 7
The Rise of the Fuhrer and the FBI

In 1932, Einstein left Germany and emigrated to America. A year later, when Hitler came to power, he once again renounced the German citizenship that he had reacquired in 1924. Albert once said that although he did not have the qualities of a man of "Jewish faith" ever since renouncing Judaism, he was happy to belong to the Jewish people and that they had come to love each other like brethren should. When Hitler was at the height of his popularity, Einstein believed it was his duty to save as many Jews as possible from his tyranny. He talked to anyone who could be influential and wrote to many organizations that were ready to help. He himself asserted that he ran a sort of immigration office, since he would recommend many refugees for United States' visas in order to try and ease the migration process. He also openly debated the importance of making immigration rules looser.

Meanwhile in Nazi Germany, two other scientists, Philipp Lenard and Johannes Stark, were trying to completely erase Einstein's work

in physics. A movement called Deutsche Physik started in Germany. It labeled Einstein's work in modern physics as "Jewish Physics" and banned it. It is said that it was this movement that delayed Germany's nuclear warhead development. Not only did many scientists flee Germany to help other countries develop it before Hitler could,

but the movement also required a lot of change in the education of young physicists. Books were rewritten and theories that could have helped its development were banned, under the label "Jewish physics".

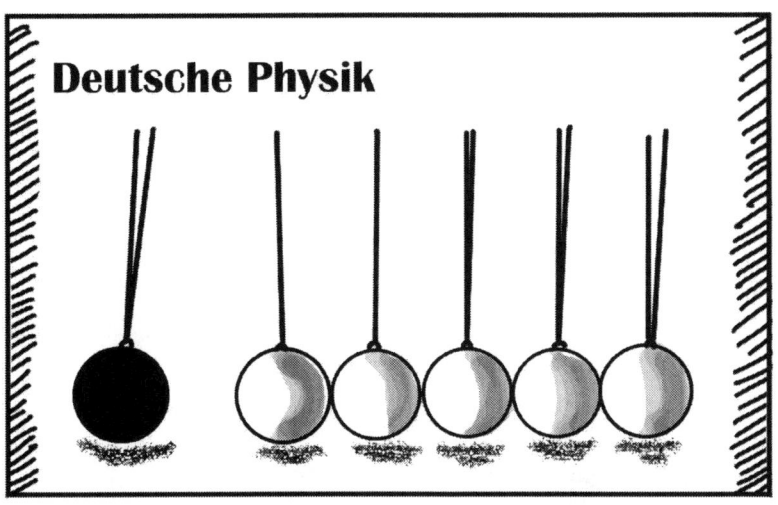

Deutsche Physik

Hitler wasted no time in putting a price of $5,000 on Einstein's head. When Albert found out, he smiled and said, "I didn't know it was worth that much". In a letter to his son, Eduard, he told him that he would probably never visit Germany again. And indeed he never did. He also refused all awards that Germany offered him in the future because he could never forgive or forget the past.

Einstein's life was not so straightforward in the United States either. He was "stalked" by the

FBI for about 22 years. It is common knowledge that the FBI has more often than not spied on famous and influential figures, be it musicians, actors or scientists. Before Einstein even set foot in the US, the first finger was pointed at him when he applied for a visa and was questioned

about his political views. This was due to a corporation which had sent the State Department a letter suggesting that Einstein had communist connections, highlighting his strong views against any sort of war or violence. Einstein lost his patience during the interview and said that he would not answer silly questions, declaring that he had been invited to the country and that if he were to enter as a suspect rather than an honorable guest, then he would rather not be there. As soon as the media unearthed this story, the State Department announced that visas for both Einstein and his wife would be issued the next day. They were and the Einsteins traveled to America in 1933.

Soon afterwards, Hitler rose to power in Germany and Einstein's stay in the US became permanent. The FBI continued to suspect him, however, mainly because his practices and beliefs seemed

illogical and were at odds with the social climate and beliefs in the US at that time. For example, they claimed that Einstein brainwashed his students into believing that individual freedom should be eliminated, that he was a member of groups that promoted violence against the government and encouraged rebellious acts. They even suggested that he was a Russian spy and was promoting communism in an attempt

HANS ALBERT EINSTEIN
1904-----1973

A LIFE DEVOTED TO HIS
STUDENT, RESEAR,-
MUSIC AND NATURE

to overthrow the government and Hollywood. All in all, they were uneasy about his support of equal rights and his anti-war approach. The FBI continued to spy on Einstein all the time he remained in America, right up until his death in 1955.

Chapter 8
Hello America!

By 1933, Einstein was one of the most renowned personalities in academic circles and at the same time the most wanted man in Nazi Germany. Hitler and his men were targeting Jews, intellectuals and pacifists and Einstein fitted into all three categories. Since he was hardly ever in Germany during Hitler's rise, he was not harmed, although, sadly, the same cannot be said about his work. The Nazis did their best to eradicate it from their academic history, even going so far as to create a whole new branch of Physics and setting fire to the existing libraries. It was clear to Einstein that it was time for a change - a change in nationality and a change in homeland. The only question was, where would they go? They started shrewdly. No one could scare Einstein, so a bold move was unnecessary and Belgium was his first solution. However, the territory under Hitler's control spread rapidly and soon Belgium was no longer a safe option. Einstein was offered a couple of jobs in the

United States and after much contemplation he finally decided that America was his ticket to the free world. He immediately found a job at the Institute for Advanced Study at Princeton and the family set sail for the US.

It was a difficult time for them all, especially now that Albert had decided to take an active part in politics. Moving to America was not easy either. At first he was not welcomed wholeheartedly because many people objected to his pacifist views, but after a little while

he and his wife were able to obtain the entry permits they needed. He earned dual Swiss and American nationality in later years (around 1940) and gave up his German citizenship again. However, due to the initial ups and downs relating to his views, he was always under inspection. Einstein and his wife helped many Jews move to America, but Einstein still had mixed feelings about being able to live a peaceful life while his Jewish brothers were being killed and the number of casualties increasing daily.

On top of all this, his beloved wife Elsa

passed away three years after they found refuge from the Nazis. At the age of 54, Albert, who had gone beyond his golden age of discovery and was now living a politically active life, was left alone to do something that did not come naturally to him - mingling with the world on his own. But however he came across to others, he loved America. He expressed this on a radio show in 1940, when he was given his citizenship. He explained that he had recently gained what people generally take for granted. It was not his new nationality that he celebrated during the broadcast, but the development of individual empowerment and creativity that came hand in hand with it. Albert considered it his "self-evident duty" to get this message through to the public. He was questioned about whether America lived up to its promise of liberty, and if that was the real reason he had chosen America as his home. Einstein replied that it was not only peace that was in question, but the freedom of

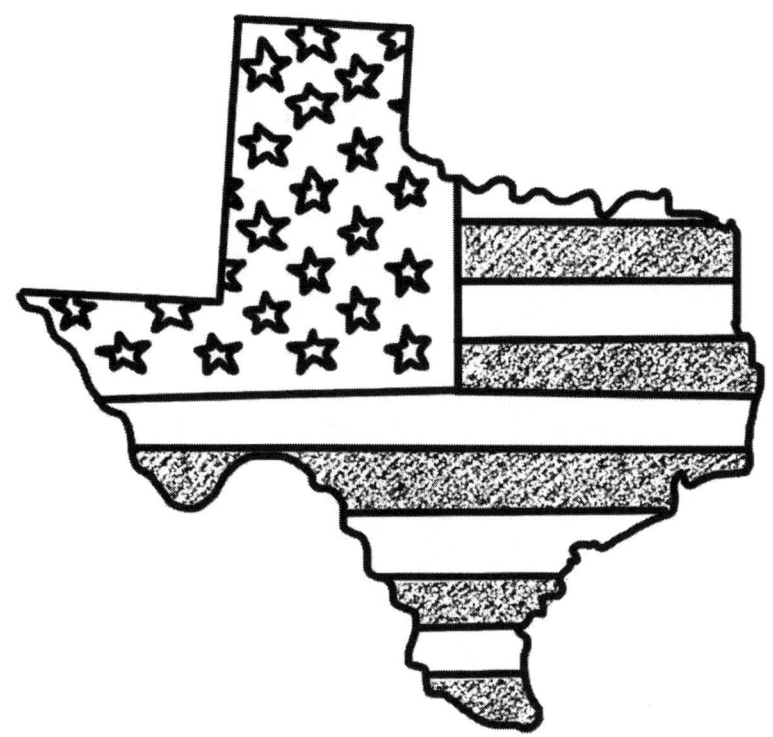

education and enlightenment. In his own words, "Without such freedom there would have been no Shakespeare, no Goethe, no Newton, no Faraday, no Pasteur, and no Lister."

Chapter 9
A Bomb Without Einstein?

It is very ironical that, throughout his lifetime, Einstein condemned warfare and violence and yet during the last decade of his life, his discoveries led to the creation of the first atomic weapon. Hence he can fairly be called the "father" of the atomic bomb. However, on his death bed, Einstein confessed to a friend that if there were anything he regretted in his life, it was the events that led to his becoming part of the Manhattan project. At the same time, there was no other way that he could see how to save people from the terror the Nazis had

unleashed onto the world. He did not participate in actually building the bomb, but was the driver behind it becoming a reality and becoming part of America's plan to defeat Hitler.

Around the end of the 1930s, German scientists had become familiar with nuclear fission in their laboratories. On a larger scale, this could be used for warfare in the form of the atomic bomb. They knew that the way to complete their abominable plans was technologically feasible for Germany. This threw the world into a frenzy of panic. If Nazi Germany developed the nuclear weapon before the rest of the world, everyone would be vulnerable. Fearing such a future, many scientists wanted to help other countries to build a bomb before Germany could. Included in the list of refugee scientists was a Hungarian

man named Leo Szilard, who wrote to President Roosevelt warning him of the world's fate, if what he and a lot of others feared actually came true. But the scientist did not have the necessary stature to gain the president's attention, so in a desperate attempt to be heard, he turned to his good friend Albert Einstein.

Einstein, who was already trying to save as many Jews as possible from Hitler's tyranny and was ready to write to anyone in power who would stand with them to fight, was easily

convinced. He signed a letter that outlined how research was needed to build a weapon from fissionable uranium, a new type of bomb for a new age, which could change the world and stop Hitler in his tracks. His letter struck a chord with the president and stirred him to action, resulting in the Manhattan project. Einstein

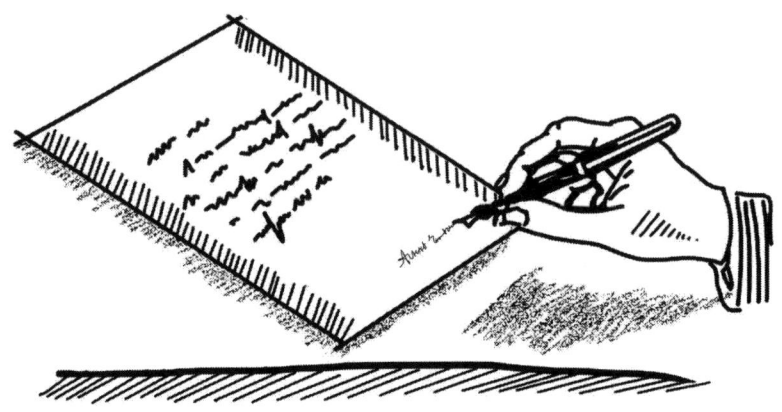

once described his "limited" involvement in a short essay, claiming that it was his letter that had achieved the desired result, even though he had no direct relationship with the project or its consequences. Indeed, without the letter there might not have been an atom bomb at all.

As it turned out, by the time America had launched its research program, the Germans had stopped theirs. So when America finally built the atom bomb in 1945, it was not only unparalleled but unnecessary, as World War II had ended and Hitler was defeated. The bombs invented to stop Hitler ended up being dropped on Japan instead.

Whatever the level of involvement, be it just a signature on a letter, Einstein's general point of view never altered. He continued to believe that warfare was not the solution, that killing during a war was no better than common killing on the street and that any war, unless

fueled by the fire of religion and its rights, was bound to end in vain. He believed that since nations will always feel the need to protect themselves, they will be compelled to build the most abominable weaponry in order to be prepared for war. He believed that such measures

only incited violence and that as long as things could be resolved peacefully, there was no need for this. In his conviction that all warfare should be abolished, he cited the example of Gandhi, saying that "the man proved that conviction is stronger than invincible material power."

Chapter 10
The Legacy of a
Legendary Physicist

In 1947, Einstein joined forces with the United Nations to make newly founded nuclear technology a way to discourage wars in the future. His perception was that if countries knew it was safe and had a proper armament program, they would remain cool-headed in the majority of situations. This would result in a diplomatic world where issues could be resolved by dialogue. Around the same time, he also joined the National Association for Advancement of Colored People. Along with many famous figures, he talked about his belief that there

was a similarity between the German Jews and African Americans in their respective countries. He strived for civil rights and, in 1946, during a speech at Lincoln University, he called racism a "disease".

Einstein always saw himself as a lone wolf and, after the death of his beloved wife, this gradually became true. After the war he had all the time he needed to devote to his work, which not only completely absorbed him but also caused him to cut himself off from scientific circles. He discussed his theories and ideas solely with his colleagues at Princeton.

But all was not lost. His beloved little sister Maja, who was also his best friend, came to live with him. Einstein would play the violin with other musicians to relive the old days when he played the instrument with his mother as a young boy. He remained a happy and

proud supporter of the recently founded state of Israel and he finally saw all the struggles being resolved. However, he voiced his concern and disagreement on witnessing the extreme violence that some Israelis inflicted on the Arabs of Palestine. Einstein was a member of the first Board of Governors of the Hebrew University of Jerusalem. He worked alongside many renowned scientists, philosophers and psychologists, such as Martin Buber and Sigmund Freud. He was offered the second presidency of Israel, which he declined, but which goes to prove his global stature and fame. He is reported to have said on one occasion, "Politics is for the moment, while an equation is for eternity." Not only was Einstein labeled the greatest Jew of his time, but he became an icon of intellect and humanitarianism.

In his last years he sailed, worked and

enjoyed life. He continued to build on his theories from home since he had retired from his post at the Institute of Advanced Study in Princeton. On his 75th birthday, he was given a parrot, which he loved dearly and enjoyed telling it jokes. But by this time the Albert Einstein who once helped a child to fix his bike while taking a walk and who

helped a young girl with her math homework at her request, was not looking after his own health. He was growing weaker and weaker every day, especially after the death of his sister in 1951, which left him lonelier than ever. But this did not stop him from playing around with the paparazzi and he would often pretend to be ill to avoid posing for photographs.

In 1955, while preparing a speech to celebrate Israel's seventh year of independence, he suffered an abdominal aortic aneurysm [the aorta, which is the largest blood vessel in the body and which leads from the heart to the stomach, swells up and can cause life-threatening bleeding if it ruptures]. Albert was instantly rushed to the University Medical Center at Princeton, where

the doctors advised surgery. But Einstein, who was against prolonging life through artificial means, refused, saying, "I want to go when I want. It's tasteless to prolong life artificially. I have done my share, it is time to go. I will do it elegantly". He passed away the next morning in the same hospital bed, at the age of 76.

Einstein the Icon

Albert Einstein was the man whose brain was indispensable even after his death. During Einstein's autopsy in Princeton Hospital a pathologist named Thomas Stoltz Harvey removed his brain within seven hours of his death, causing general, and not only scientific, speculation. Harvey cut the brain into several pieces, keeping a few for himself and giving the rest to other pathologists for them to try and unlock the secrets of this brilliant mind. Whether or not Einstein's brain was removed with his consent is still a matter of dispute. His elder son Hans gave his permission after the event had already taken place, with the objective of aiding scientific research and progress.

However, the studies showed no significant result. It was observed that the areas involving speech and language were smaller than those responsible for numerical processing. Harvey also took out Einstein's eyes and gave them to the latter's ophthalmologist.

Einstein's remains were cremated and his ashes were spread in a secret location, according to his wishes. Some say it was at the Institute of Advanced Study at Princeton. His brain was later given to the National Museum of Health and Medicine by Thomas Harvey's heirs.

Even after his death, Albert Einstein's fame and status as an evergreen symbol of wisdom grew. The mad professor with the unruly white hair still lives on. In our books, in our memes, on our t-shirts and bumper stickers.

His life changed not only the realm of physics but affected billions of people around the globe.

EinStein'S Timeline

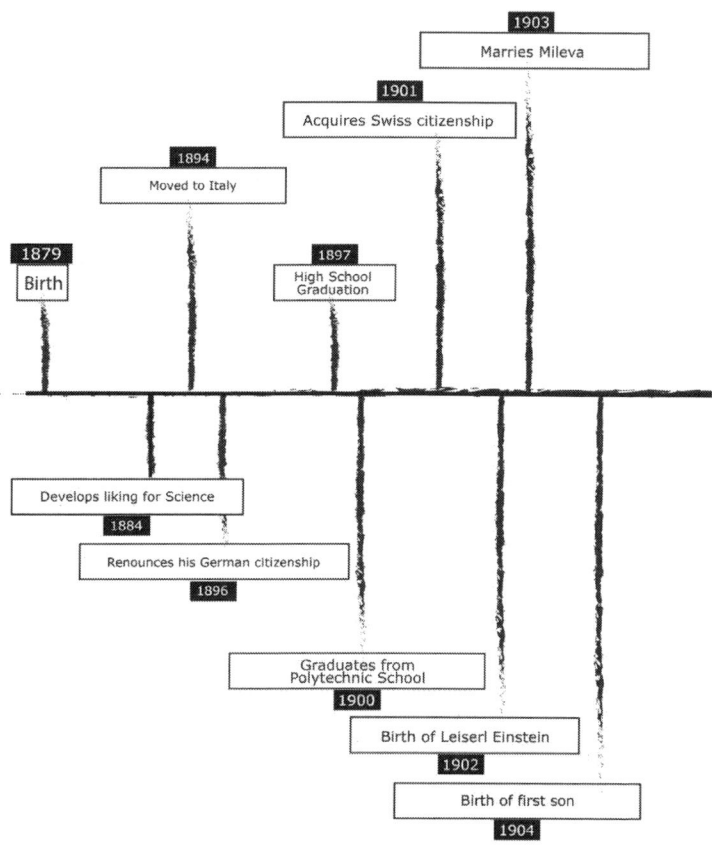

1903
Marries Mileva

1901
Acquires Swiss citizenship

1894
Moved to Italy

1879
Birth

1897
High School Graduation

Develops liking for Science
1884

Renounces his German citizenship
1896

Graduates from Polytechnic School
1900

Birth of Leiserl Einstein
1902

Birth of first son
1904

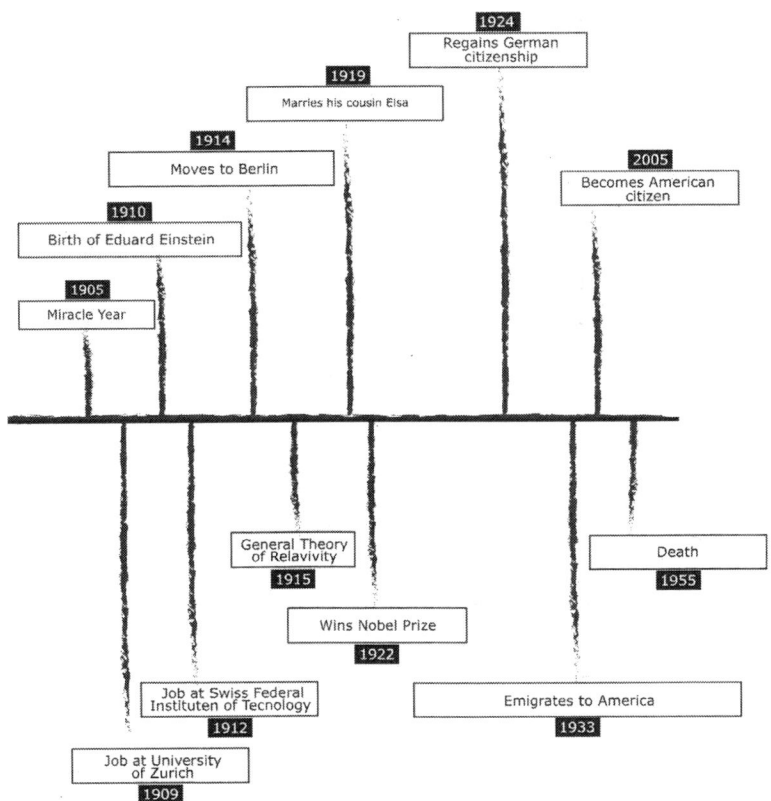

1924
Regains German citizenship

1919
Marries his cousin Elsa

1914
Moves to Berlin

1910
Birth of Eduard Einstein

2005
Becomes American citizen

1905
Miracle Year

General Theory of Relavivity
1915

Death
1955

Wins Nobel Prize
1922

Job at Swiss Federal Instituten of Tecnology
1912

Emigrates to America
1933

Job at University of Zurich
1909

Bibliography

1987-1996, Princeton. "The Collected Papers of Albert Einstein, Volume 1-6." Princeton. *The Collected Papers of Albert Einstein.* Editors: R. Schulmann, 1987-1996. volumes 1-6.

"Nobel Lectures ." *Nobel Lectures, Physics 1901-1921* (1967). website .

website, Team Einstein. *http://www.einstein-website.de.* n.d.

Shmoop Editorial Team. "Albert Einstein: Last Years & Death." *Shmoop. Shmoop* University, Inc., 11 Nov. 2008. Web. 15 Jan. 2017.

62471004R00058

Made in the USA
Lexington, KY
08 April 2017